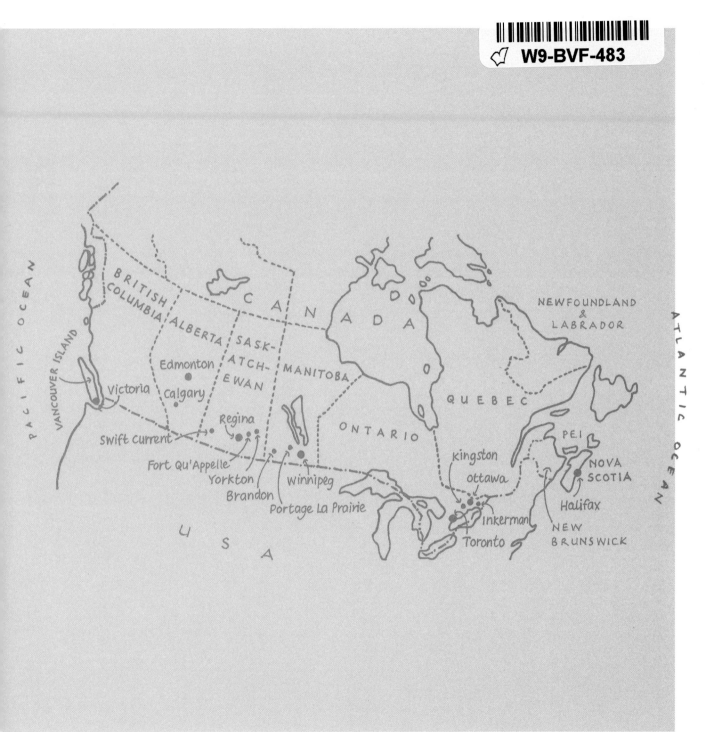

Charlie

Charlie

A Home Child's Life in Canada

BERYL YOUNG

KEY PORTER BOOKS

Library and Archives Canada Cataloguing in Publication

Young, Beryl, 1934-
    Charlie : a home child's life in Canada / Beryl Young.

ISBN 978-1-55470-200-8

1. Harvey, Charlie—Juvenile literature. 2. Home children (Canadian immigrants)—Biography—Juvenile literature. 3. Royal Canadian Mounted Police—Biography—Juvenile literature. 4. Police—Canada—Biography—Juvenile literature. 5. Canada. Canadian Army. Canadian Expeditionary Force—Biography—Juvenile literature. I. Title.

HV7911.H37Y68 2009   j363.2092   C2009-902106-4

ONTARIO ARTS COUNCIL
CONSEIL DES ARTS DE L'ONTARIO

The publisher gratefully acknowledges the support of the Canada Council for the Arts and the Ontario Arts Council for its publishing program. We acknowledge the support of the Government of Ontario through the Ontario Media Development Corporation's Ontario Book Initiative.

We acknowledge the financial support of the Government of Canada through the Book Publishing Industry Development Program (BPIDP) for our publishing activities.

Key Porter Books Limited
Six Adelaide Street East, Tenth Floor
Toronto, Ontario
Canada M5C 1H6

www.keyporter.com

Endpaper maps: Michelle Buhl-Nielson
Text design: Sonya V. Thursby
Electronic formatting: Sonya V. Thursby

Printed and bound in Canada

09 10 11 12 13 5 4 3 2 1

For my brother Bob,
who also wanted to know the story,
and for our cousin Phyllis,
who helped find it.

CONTENTS

INTRODUCTION
Home Children

Charlie Harvey was one of 100,000 young British children sent to Canada between 1860 and 1934. These girls and boys—usually between the ages of eight and fourteen—were called Home Children because in England they had lived in safe shelters, like orphanages, which were known as Homes.

One of the most famous of these was Barnardo's Home. It was named after Dr. Thomas Barnardo, a man who rescued thousands of abandoned children from the streets of London. He provided them with food and shelter, schooling, and training in trades. In time, Barnardo's Homes began to accept children like Charlie, who was not orphaned but whose only parent was unable to care for him.

There was much poverty in Britain, particularly in London. So many children needed shelter that the Homes became overcrowded quickly. People like Dr. Barnardo struggled with an important question: Where could these children go? Where would they have a chance for a good future? They looked to Canada, which was then part of the British Empire. Canada was a healthy place to live and was badly in need of farm workers. So it was that shiploads of children began to arrive on Canada's eastern shores on their way to placement in farms and homes. Some of these children were treated cruelly and their lives were difficult, but for many others who were welcomed and treated kindly, life in Canada was good.

Showing courage, commitment, and a capacity for hard work, most Home Children went on to lead successful lives as productive citizens in all professions, making a significant contribution in every part of Canada.

Charlie Harvey was my father and this is his story. If I could ask him now, I know he'd say that being a Home Child gave him an extraordinary opportunity to have the kind of life he'd never have had in England. In writing this book, I regretted that there were many questions I never asked him. I hope the story I've woven around the known facts brings his experience to life.

It is estimated that the children, grandchildren, and great grandchildren of Home Children number more than 12 percent of the people in Canada today. That means four million Canadians are descendants of Home Children.

I am proud to be one of them. Maybe some of you are too. ✳

ONE

A Family Torn Apart

Charlie Harvey was just thirteen years old when his father died of pneumonia. It was the fall of 1910 and his family was living on Canton Street in Southampton, a large shipping port in the south of England. The Harveys lived in rented rooms above the sweet shop where Charlie's father worked. With nine people in the family, it was crowded, but there was always lots of laughter and fun among the children. His mother always said they were poor because his father gave away too much candy, but Charlie never remembered feeling poor. He did remember his father's big grin as he slipped sweets across the counter to Charlie, his little brother Arthur, and his four sisters, Eva, Hilda, Freda, and Edie. Charlie's favourite candies were the striped, brown humbugs and his sisters loved the yellow pear drops, but four-year-old Arthur, the only member of the family with blue eyes, was crazy about huge gobstoppers, and was forever pulling one out of his mouth with sticky fingers to show how the colours changed when he sucked through the layers.

Charlie's father, Charles, worked hard all day in the shop, and to make the extra money his family needed, he took a second job in the evenings as an attendant at a large pool downtown where people came for massages and steam baths. Coming home late one rainy night, Charles caught a cold. Three days later, he was terribly ill with pneumonia. Charlie's mother told Hilda to run for a doctor, but by the time an out-of-breath Hilda returned, it was too late. Charlie's father had died.

Charlie's newest sister, Nellie, was just three months old when her father died, and for days afterwards all Charlie's mother did was hold the baby and cry. Charlie couldn't believe what had happened. He felt he was too old to cry, but his big sisters and Arthur did. As the days went by, Charlie noticed that Arthur stuck close to him, looking up with those intense blue eyes and holding onto Charlie's pant legs as though his big brother could take the place of their father. Charlie decided he'd always make time to kick around a soccer ball with his brother, and every night he'd let Arthur curl up beside him in bed while Charlie talked him to sleep. Arthur was small for his age and his little legs would push out in his sleep. Charlie had to be patient and shift to the other side of the bed. Still, Arthur would slide after him and squeeze his warm body against his brother's back for comfort.

Life without their father was a big adjustment, but Charlie soon learned that more changes were coming. Without her husband's earnings, Charlie's mother, Sarah, had only six shillings a week from the church widows' fund, and with all the children to feed and her savings spent on the funeral, she decided to move her family from the flat above the sweet shop into two rooms in a nearby house. Because money was scarce, the older girls were sent to find jobs. Sixteen-year-old Eva went to work as a chambermaid in a London hotel and Hilda, who was fourteen, became a domestic servant in the home of a wealthy Southampton ship owner.

A Difficult Decision

The departure of Eva and Hilda meant that Charlie was now the oldest child at home. It was a cold autumn and there wasn't enough money to keep coal in the stove. Some nights, even with Eva and Hilda sending their wages to their mother, the children at home had nothing more than plain bread with their evening tea. Charlie got a job selling newspapers on the street. He was a handsome boy and the customers liked him, but the fivepence he earned a week wasn't enough to make a difference. One day, two months after her husband had died, Sarah called the children around the kitchen table and told them that without their father to earn a living she could no longer keep the family together. His mother was only thirty-eight years old, but to Charlie she looked exhausted as she explained the decision to put them in orphanages.

The children sat in silence as their mother told them that a girls' orphanage in Southampton had accepted curly-haired, ten-year-old Freda and carefree Edie, almost seven. Arthur, the youngest boy, would go to Fegan's Home for Boys in a town called Stony Stratford about ninety miles to the north. She planned to keep baby Nellie with her and take in laundry at sixpence a load. Charlie waited impatiently for his mother to say he'd be going with Arthur.

English Money

In the early 1900s in England, a penny—written as 1d and called a pence—was a small copper coin. A farthing was an even smaller copper coin, worth a quarter of a penny. Arthur's gobstoppers would have cost a farthing. For a halfpenny, which was pronounced as "hayp'ny", you could buy a handful of broken biscuits from a shop.

Charlie's mother could earn sixpence a day by taking in laundry, which would be about three cents in today's Canadian money. Twelvepence made a shilling—a silver coin. Charlie's father might have earned as much as thirty-two shillings a week. Twenty shillings made a pound (£), which was a green paper note. It would have been rare for the children in Charlie's family to have seen many pound notes.

Instead, she told him that Fegan's accepted only boys from three to ten years old. Because he was thirteen, Charlie would be travelling with a kind neighbour, Miss Rooke, to a Dr. Barnardo's Home in London, where they took older boys. Hearing that he'd be separated from his big brother, Arthur's face collapsed and he began to howl.

Charlie was furious. He told his mother he wouldn't leave Arthur, who was now clinging to him and soaking his pant leg with tears. But his mother just shook her head and said she had no other choice. She put the baby to bed and began to cook an especially nice supper. That night every member of the family had a whole egg with their bread.

Once the younger children were asleep, Charlie went to his mother where she was cleaning the ashes from the stove and begged her not to send him away. He'd get a job helping at the local dairy or in the shipyards; he'd do anything to stay. Sarah sat down beside her oldest boy and took his hand. She told him that putting her children in orphanages was the most difficult thing she'd ever had to do. She loved her children dearly, she said, and was trying to do what was right for them.

His mother looked intently at Charlie. She said she'd thought hard about the best place for him and had decided on a Home founded by Dr. Barnardo who was famous for helping orphaned children. His Homes also took in children, like Charlie, who couldn't be cared for by a single parent.

Sarah told Charlie that Dr. Barnardo had died seven years earlier but that his Homes were still sending children to work on farms in Canada. You are very lucky, she told Charlie. Next year, when you are fourteen, you'll be eligible to go too.

Charlie was puzzled. Why would his mother want him to go so far away from England? He'd never thought much about Canada. All he knew was that it was part of the British Empire and was thousands of miles across the Atlantic Ocean. Seeing the look on her son's face, Sarah ruffled Charlie's dark hair and smiled to reassure him. Canada would be a fresh start in a new country, she said, with opportunities he'd never find in England. And maybe one day Arthur could join him.

As Charlie sat looking down at his hands, trying to take in what his mother had said, Sarah went to a drawer and came back with a metal bottle opener. It was nothing special, just a small black tool, but Charlie had often seen his father use it to open his favourite ginger beer. Sarah passed the bottle opener to her eldest son, saying it was all she had for him. He was to take the opener with him as a reminder that he was not a real orphan—he had a mother who would always love him. Charlie looked at his mother's pained face and clenched the opener so tightly the sharp point hurt his hand. He was still upset, but he wouldn't argue anymore.

☞ The bottle opener that belonged to Charlie's dad, given to Charlie by his mother the night before he left for Barnardo's.

Dr. Thomas Barnardo

John Thomas Barnardo was the best known of many people who cared about the plight of poor children in the 1800s in England. In his lifetime, he helped thousands of boys and girls, and because he believed in providing them with a new start in Canada, he also greatly increased the British influence in Canada.

Born in Dublin, Ireland, in 1845, Thomas had a cruel schoolmaster he never forgot. At the age of seventeen he converted to the evangelical branch of the Plymouth Brethren church and studied medicine in London. His chance meeting with a London street urchin called Jim Jarvis changed the life of thousands of English children (see "The Story of Jim Jarvis" on page 18).

So many abandoned children began arriving at his first Home that one night Thomas Barnardo was forced to turn a desperate boy away. When the boy was later found dead of exposure and starvation, a sorrowful Dr. Barnardo decided he'd never again turn away a needy child. He had a sign made to go over the doorway of the Home: No Destitute Child Ever Refused Admission.

With his waxed moustache and penetrating eyes, Dr. Barnardo was a familiar figure around London. He was a dapper five feet, three inches tall and always wore a silk top hat to make himself appear taller. His fiery speeches made him a popular preacher and attracted thousand of people to support the growing number of Homes he set up around London.

At Dr. Barnardo's, the boys were kept busy from dawn to dusk. Thomas felt that every child should learn a trade, but he always made certain they had time for music,

☞ Dr. Barnardo was a kind man who helped thousands of British children.

exercise and play. He would never allow any of the children to be beaten or harmed.

Thomas married a schoolteacher who encouraged him to help homeless girls by setting up a Girls' village. House mothers trained the girls to cook, sew, and clean so they could find employment in hotels and private houses.

With thousands of children in his care in more than a 110 Homes, Dr. Barnardo needed to find a place for the older children to go. Along with other benefactors of the time he came to believe that sending children to work on farms in Canada would give them a better future than they'd ever have in England (see "Why Canada" on page 29).

Dr. Barnardo set high standards for the children selected to travel. He insisted that they be healthy, have sharp eyesight, and good teeth. "Only the flower of the flock," he claimed, would be allowed to emigrate. Between 1869 and 1930 Dr. Barnardo's organization alone sent more than 30,000 girls and boys to Canada. There were criticisms of this policy as well as his administration of the Homes, but Dr. Barnardo weathered them all.

Dr. Barnardo visited Canada several times before he died in 1905. His work has been carried on for many years, and today the organization that still bears his name has many programs to help children and families (see "Barnardo's Today" on page 104).

One night in the autumn of 1870, after the young Dr. Barnardo had been preaching in an east London hall, he came out onto the street and saw a thin boy in ragged clothes, barefoot and shivering in the dark. He told the boy, who looked about ten, that it was late and he should go home to his mother, but the boy answered that he had no mother.

Then show me where you live, Dr. Barnardo said. The boy told him that he'd lived on the street since his mother had died when he was five.

But where did you sleep last night? Dr. Barnardo asked, finding it hard to believe.

Jim Jarvis led Dr. Barnardo to a shed in an alleyway. The man shone his lantern inside and was shocked to see a ragged group of boys sleeping with their heads on piles of hay and their feet in the gutter. Jim told him there were boys like this all over London.

☞ Many boys like Jim Jarvis were left to make their way on the London streets.

That night Jim stayed with Dr. Barnardo, and in a few short weeks the compassionate preacher had opened up a home for thirty-three boys, most of them between the ages of thirteen and fourteen. The boys were given haircuts and clean clothes, fed regular meals, and put to work chopping wood to earn money for their keep.

Jim Jarvis was one of the first boys to be sent to Canada. Dr. Barnardo always credited Jim with starting his lifelong mission to provide a future for thousands of children.

Going Away

The very next morning, the family walked Arthur the mile along city streets and through the busy town centre to the Southampton train station. The usually noisy girls were quiet and Arthur kept a tight hold on his big brother's hand. On the platform the little boy refused to take the bag his mother had packed for him, clutching first to his mother and then to Charlie. Charlie put on a brave face as he squeezed Arthur's narrow shoulders and bent to whisper a promise that they'd be together again one day. The sight of his small brother's miserable face staring out the smudged train window tore at Charlie's heart.

Later that day, Charlie put his father's bottle opener in with the few clothes he'd packed and was ready when Miss Rooke came to take him on the train. He kissed his mother as she stood on the street surrounded by her girls with the baby in her arms. Tears streamed down everyone's faces and baby Nellie cried her heart out. Charlie stared straight in front of him. He was thirteen. He had to be ready for whatever lay ahead. *

☞ Trains led Arthur and Charlie to their new lives away from one another.

TWO

One of Dr. Barnardo's Boys

As the train pulled out of the South-ampton station, Charlie had a shaky feeling in his stomach. Part of it, he knew, came from nerves, but part of it was something else. He couldn't help feeling a bit excited. Here he was, sitting on the upholstered train seat beside Miss Rooke on his very first train ride. He was on his way to London, the capital of England! It was fascinating to look out the window, watching villages and tidy fields pass by and later seeing row upon row of brick houses that signalled the outskirts of the big city of London. Then he began to feel guilty. He was leaving his entire family behind. His mother would be alone with Nellie. How could he feel excited at all?

After a two-hour trip, the train pulled into Waterloo, an enormous glass-topped railway station in the heart of London. Miss Rooke led Charlie outside and they caught one of the new, red, electric trams, built with two levels to carry many passengers. Charlie made Miss Rooke climb to the top deck where they had a good view of the city. They passed Buckingham Palace, the tall grey home of King George V, the grandson of Queen Victoria. Once again, the excited feeling returned. Buckingham Palace! What would Arthur have to say about that? Charlie wondered how soon he'd have a chance to tell his brother about this trip.

By the time Charlie got off the tram in Stepney, on the east side of London, the nervous feeling was back. Miss Rooke led him across the road to a large, dark building, surrounded by a wall that made it look like a prison. They walked around the corner and up steep steps to the front door.

☞ Charlie's first look at Leopold House.
The high wall made it seem like a prison.

Above the door was a sign:

LEOPOLD HOUSE
DR. BARNARDO'S BOYS' HOME
NO DESTITUTE CHILD EVER
REFUSED ADMISSION

Inside, they were greeted by a tall matron who nodded to Charlie and asked Miss Rooke to fill out a form. Miss Rooke wrote quickly, gave Charlie a nervous smile, and kissed him goodbye on his cheek. Then she turned him toward the matron who peered down at him through thick, round glasses. Charlie followed the matron's sweeping skirt, their footsteps echoing through the empty halls, to a small room. The matron pointed to a bench and told Charlie to sit so his photograph could be taken.

Charlie had never seen a camera before. He stared at the large box sitting on a tripod and waited, wondering how on earth the contraption managed to create the likenesses he'd seen in shop windows. Eventually another boy about his age came into the room, made some adjustments to the back of the large box, then looked at Charlie, and winked. The boy ducked his head under a black cloth covering the camera, there was a flash, and the boy's head popped out again. It was amazing that someone his own age knew how to take photographs. As Charlie followed the matron out of the room, the boy winked at him again.

Next, Charlie was weighed on a tall scale. Sixty-six pounds, the matron said in a tone that suggested she thought Charlie was small for his age. She handed him a bundle containing black pants, a white shirt, black boots and a jacket, and led him upstairs to the dormitory. It was a long room with high windows and a row of narrow beds down each side. Pointing to a bed at the end of the room, the matron told Charlie to put on the clothes and wait for the dinner whistle.

Afternoon light strained through the dirty glass windows onto the beds, each one covered with a grey blanket. Charlie counted. Twenty beds. At home, he and

Arthur and often Edie had slept together in one big bed. He dressed and sat on the bed with his arms hanging between his knees, trying to get used to the stiff jacket and the tight boots. Before long he heard the stomping of boys and they streamed into the room, all in identical uniforms. Few gave him a passing glance before talking or pulling out cards to play with their friends. Charlie was certain he'd never fit in.

At the sound of a shrill whistle half an hour later, the boys headed out the door and rushed noisily back down the stairs. Charlie followed them into a high-ceilinged hall with long wooden tables and benches. He stood beside the other boys while a stern-looking master in a dark suit said grace. "For what we are about to receive, may the Lord make us truly thankful. Amen."

Charlie joined the scramble onto benches that scraped across the wood floors. Boys who were servers brought soup, bread, and tea to each table. Eating was quick, with no talking and no second helpings. Then, with a word from the master, the boys filed out to a bare yard without a single tree or a blade of grass. This was free time for them to play soccer or crouch in groups for games of jacks.

Charlie leaned his back against the courtyard's high brick wall. The big city of London was just on the other side. He could hear the noisy trams going by. The King and Queen were not far away in their grand palace. His sister Eva was working at a hotel in some part of the city, and here he was in a dirt yard with a pack of street orphans. He wasn't even one of them; he'd just had the bad luck to have a father who'd become sick and died. It wasn't fair! His mother had made a mistake sending him here.

At Leopold House, the lights-out whistle blew at eight o'clock sharp, and for the first time in his life Charlie had a bed to himself, however narrow and hard. He put on the nightshirt, pulled up the scratchy blanket and lay staring at the ceiling. He missed squirmy little Arthur and wondered how his brother was doing at Fegan's orphanage. Was the poor little fellow feeling alone and scared in a dormitory with unfriendly boys? After a long while, Charlie fell asleep to the rustling and shifting of the other boys in the big room.

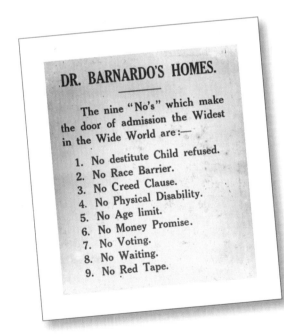

A Whistle Rules the Day

Every day at Leopold House started with a sharp whistle at six in the morning. The boys washed and dressed and made their beds, pulling the blanket so tight that a penny could bounce on it. Charlie tried to do the same. A second whistle announced breakfast. Standing beside the long table, the boys sang "God Save the King" and after grace was said, sat down to bowls of porridge with lots of milk and molasses. Here, in his new home, grace was beginning to mean something to Charlie. He was truly thankful for the good food he was receiving at Dr. Barnardo's.

After breakfast, another whistle signalled one group of boys to wash dishes, others to clean the bathrooms and wipe down the floors.

☞ The Nine No's at Barnardo's. Dr. Barnardo was very liberal in his views.

The next whistle announced that it was time for the boys to go out to the yard for physical exercises, and another whistle began two hours of school. Charlie was good at reading and writing; he liked the reading master who complimented him on his fine handwriting. After the noon meal, which was always a feast of meat and potatoes, the whistle sent boys to different parts of the big building where they were taught trades. Dr. Barnardo had insisted that his boys have practical skills, and at Leopold House they chose between making shoes, tailoring, carpentry, or learning to set type in the print shop. Charlie picked carpentry, and found he enjoyed making bookends and small cabinets out of wood.

☞ Boys exercising in the yard at Leopold House. Dr. Barnardo stressed the importance of fresh air and exercise.

☞ Learning skills in the carpentry class at Leopold House. Dr Barnardo believed the boys should have a trade.

Music was also very important to Dr. Barnardo, and boys who were musical by nature were encouraged to join the choir or learn to play an instrument in the band. Charlie decided not to join either one, but he did enjoy singing hymns after the evening meal, called tea. Every Sunday there was church with more singing and a sermon by the distinguished grey-haired governor, and for Sunday tea, three sandwiches and a piece of cake in place of the usual soup and bread.

The days at Leopold House were busy. No matter what the weather, there was an hour twice a day in the yard for exercises and games, school classes every morning and study every night, with every change of activity controlled by the commanding whistle. Still, there was time for Charlie to make a few friends and hear their stories. He liked Peter, the boy who had winked at him while taking his photograph, best. Peter had been looked after by his grandmother until she died, and had survived alone in her house for weeks until a neighbour had taken him to Dr. Barnardo's. Peter told Charlie he was happy at Barnardo's, and that certainly seemed to be true. Peter liked to joke around and was always playing tricks, hiding one of Charlie's boots or teasing that the matron was looking for him.

Charlie also made friends with a younger boy called Will, who was a whiz at jacks. Will had been left on the doorstep of Leopold House as a baby and knew nothing of his background. He'd been given the last name of Found because he was a foundling. Learning the stories about his new friends made Charlie realize how lucky he was. He may be separated from his family, but at least he still had one.

His mother wrote once a week telling him that even though the girls were close by, she wasn't allowed to visit them. Their orphanage in Southampton had a policy of no visits, saying the children became too upset after seeing their mothers. Once, his mother wrote, she'd stood outside the orphanage fence trying to catch a glimpse of Freda and Edie in the playground and one of the supervisors had chased her away. She hadn't heard from Arthur. He was too young to write and she had no money to buy a train ticket to visit him. The baby, Nellie, was sitting up and eating porridge now. Be a good boy, his mother wrote, and remember you will have a fine future when you go to Canada. Charlie wrote back telling his mother about the good food and that he'd made two friends. He didn't tell her that the lights out whistle was a signal for him to lie awake worrying about Arthur,

Why Canada?

In the early 1800s, the Industrial Revolution brought enormous changes to Britain. Many farm workers left the countryside to work in factories with the new power-driven machines. In large cities like London, overcrowded housing, low wages, and large families lead to increasing poverty. Many children were abandoned.

The time was ripe for people like Dr. Barnardo, who cared about the plight of these children, to open safe shelters. To keep the doors open for more and more children, however, there had to be a place for the older children to go.

Canada was considered perfect because it was not heavily industrialized or overcrowded. Its wide open spaces would be a healthy environment for British children.

As well, Canada was a part of the British Empire and much closer to England than Australia and New Zealand. The new steamships crossing the Atlantic Ocean were an inexpensive and safe way for the children to travel. The Canadian government, seeing a chance to obtain low-cost workers, welcomed the idea of child immigrants. So did Canadian farmers desperate for help on their land.

Charlie and the other children who sailed to Canada in 1911 were just a fraction of the 2,524 children sent to Canada that year.

☞ Girls as well as boys were given a chance to start a new life in Canada.

wondering if his little brother had found a friend who'd appreciate his funny ways.

A Surprise Announcement

One morning early in the New Year, after just five months at Barnardo's, Charlie was called to the governor's office. Had he done something wrong? The tall man sat at his desk and motioned Charlie to sit across from him. Charlie couldn't control the shaking in his legs. The governor looked up from his papers and announced that even though Charlie wouldn't be fourteen until August, he'd passed a medical test and been chosen as one of 217 boys who would sail to Canada on February 25. The children would sail aboard the SS *Sicilian*, a steamer owned by the Allan Line.

Charlie's heart raced with the news. This was it. This is what his mother had wanted for him, a chance to make a life far away in Canada. But it was happening so soon! The governor explained that Miss Rooke had signed the form with his mother's permission for him to leave Canada. He could barely take in the words as the governor stood and reached out to shake his hand. Work hard and learn all you can, he said. There are great opportunities waiting in the new land.

Over the next few weeks, the boys training as tailors sewed each traveller two coarse, black cloth suits. They were to wear one outfit with boots, suspenders and a cap; the better suit was packed in a small wooden trunk along with two nightshirts, woolen socks, a pair of work overalls big enough to grow into, a boot brush, needles and wool to repair the socks, and the Bible. Charlie added his father's bottle opener, tucking it safely inside the pocket of his good suit jacket.

Charlie knew this was what his mother wanted. But he'd be crossing the Atlantic ocean, and he needed to say goodbye. It was devastating to learn that he wouldn't be allowed to see any of his family before he left. He was heading to a strange country— a far away continent—and there would be no chance to hug his mother, no chance to explain to Arthur why he was leaving so soon. Some small part of Charlie couldn't help but be thrilled about the adventure ahead, but his heart was heavy at the thought of going so far away.

There was time for a haircut and a departure photograph in his new suit. Charlie sat on the same bench he'd sat on his first day at Dr. Barnardo's, and this time Peter fooled around behind the black cloth, trying to make Charlie laugh and spoil the picture. Charlie managed to look serious in the photograph, which showed that his hair was shorter and he'd put on some weight since coming to Barnardo's. Watching Peter's antics, Charlie realized just how much he'd miss his new friend. Since his father's death, life had been full of goodbyes. ✳

☞ Charlie just before he left Barnardo's to sail to Canada. What adventures lie ahead?

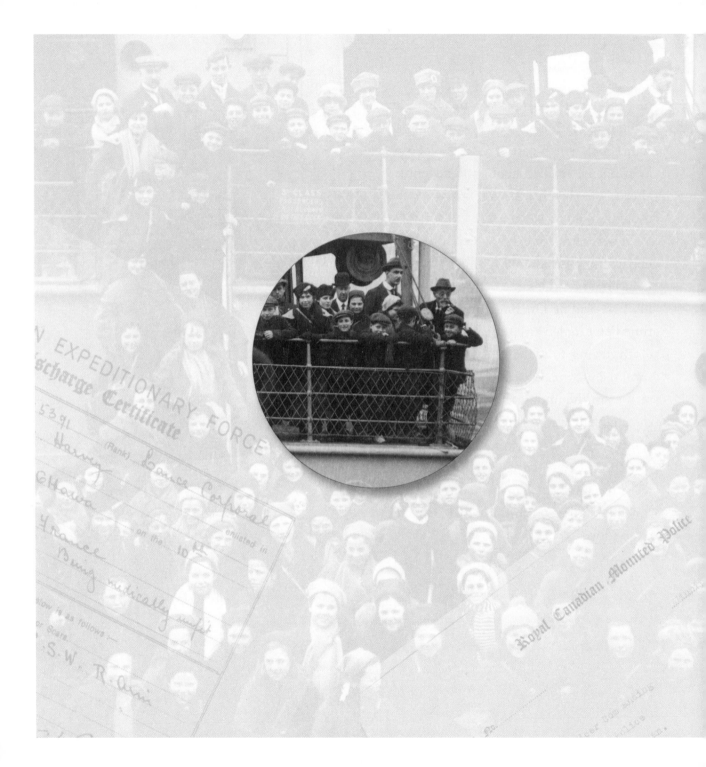

THREE

The Golden Bridge

The boys were high-spirited as they boarded the train to Liverpool, pushing and shoving each other, excited to sail on a big ship across the Atlantic. At the dock Charlie had his first look at the enormous SS *Sicilian*, with the Union Jack, Britain's flag, fluttering at its stern. The boys were soon joined by 113 equally enthusiastic Barnardo girls, wearing hats and long coats.

The governor of Leopold House made a speech, telling the young men and women that Dr. Barnardo had once described the Atlantic crossing as "a golden bridge, with one pier resting in the gloom of darkest England the other set among the limitless possibilities of the great Colonial Empire." Prayers were said for the safety of the Home Children, and as they marched up the gangplank to board the ship, the boys' band from Leopold House played a rousing version of "Land of Hope and Glory." The words resounded with each step Charlie took.

Land of Hope and Glory
Mother of the Free
How shall we extol thee,
Who are born of thee?
Wider still and wider
Shall thy bounds be set;
God who made thee mighty,
Make thee mightier yet.

Did the song mean that by going to Canada Charlie was helping to set wider bounds for England? He was too small to make his country mighty. He was thirteen, too young, he felt, to make any difference to anyone. As he stood on the deck watching

☞ The adventure begins as the SS *Sicilian*
leaves the dock at Liverpool sailing for
Canada.

the shores of England grow more and more distant, Charlie felt adrift. He was leaving his mother, Arthur and his sisters far behind. He might never see them again. He had a jittery feeling in his stomach, but whether it was from fear or excitement he couldn't tell.

As the SS *Sicilian* sailed out of the harbour, the adult guardian accompanying the group led the boys along the deck and down steep stairs to the steerage compartments. In each low-ceilinged cabin there were four deep tiers of wooden bunks, enough for sixty boys. A coal stove stood against the bulkhead at the far end of each room. Charlie grabbed a lower bunk and stowed his trunk underneath. He was grateful that the small bunk was warm and dry, but he quickly discovered that it was no refuge from the motion of the sea.

As the ship reached deeper waters, giant Atlantic swells sent the boat heeling from one side to the other. The rolling got steeper and steeper, and the boat shuddered like a wet dog shaking itself. Charlie's queasiness soon turned to vomiting. He hated it when he didn't make it down the hallway to the toilet, and he hated it when he came staggering back to the sleeping room where the smell of soiled sheets made him sick all over again. The constant thumping from the engine room next to the steerage compartment went on twenty-four hours a day. Beat for beat it matched the pounding in Charlie's head.

"All Out!"

Every day, no matter how rough the seas, their guardian insisted that each boy obey the "All out!" call.

Even feeling sick, Charlie was forced to get up, dress, wash, and sit at a table for prayers and breakfast. The crew dished food onto the children's tin plates, and at first Charlie couldn't keep anything in his stomach. After a few days he felt a little better and could at least pick at the food—sausages and eggs, fried tripe and onions—all of which would have been a feast on solid land.

Eventually Charlie was well enough and he ventured up on deck with the others. It was a relief to breathe fresh air, feel the cool wind on his face, and lean against the railing to watch the sparkling surf crest along the tops of the big roller waves. The Barnardo girls were out on deck too, the wind blowing their coats against their legs, their long hair whipping out behind them. On the deck above, the first-class passengers could be seen taking their daily walks. Laughing men and women wore coats trimmed with fur, looking warm and rich, while music from live bands drifted onto the deck below. Charlie imagined their fancy dining room and the private staterooms with clean sheets on the beds.

In the middle of its seventh night at sea, the *Sicilian* ran straight into a fierce storm. The boat began to corkscrew forward and backward as well as pitch from side to side, and Charlie's awful seasickness returned, worse than ever. In the dark cabins, boys huddled in their bunks crying for their mothers. The smell of urine and vomit and the pounding of the engine ground into Charlie's head until he wished he'd never heard of Canada. It took two days for the seas to calm, and when Charlie finally went up on deck again the ship was surrounded by a thick fog. It was eerily quiet, as though the ship was invisible and would float on forever and never be found. It was like being in a dream, only he was awake.

When the fog cleared, one of the boys spotted three whales close to the ship and everyone ran over to stare at the large creatures. Charlie loved the whales, marvelling at how gracefully they moved through the huge waves. As the ship plowed its way closer to North America the children began to spot icebergs, the floating giants they'd heard about as the most dangerous threat to ships crossing the Atlantic at that time of year.

On the morning of March 10, in dense fog, the SS *Sicilian* pulled alongside the dock at Halifax, Nova Scotia. After thirteen days at sea, Charlie had arrived in Canada. ✳

The Sinking of the *Titanic*

Charlie was right to be worried that the SS *Sicilian* might hit an iceberg. On the same route, just thirteen months after his own 1911 voyage, the RMS *Titanic* struck an iceberg and sank 400 miles off the coast of Newfoundland.

The British Star Line who built the *Titanic* boasted that not only was she the largest ship in the world but she was unsinkable because they'd built the ship with water tight bulkhead compartments.

The ship left Southampton, England, on her maiden voyage April 10, 1912. On the night of April 14, the ship hit an iceberg that ripped a long gash along the starboard hull. Water poured over the supposedly watertight bulkheads. The Captain ordered the crew to send radio SOS signals and to fire distress flares into the sky.

☞ Many artists have been inspired to paint the tragic sinking of the *Titanic*.

As terrified women and children scrambled into lifeboats, it became obvious that the company had not supplied enough lifeboats for the 2,228 passengers. Within two and a half hours the ship upended and sank.

Only 705 passengers and crew survived the sinking of the "unsinkable" *Titanic*. More than 1,500 people perished.

The remains of the *Titanic* were not found until 1985, lying two miles deep on the ocean floor. You can read about Dr. Robert Ballard's exciting discovery on the web.

FOUR

The New Land

The "All out!" was called for the last time and Charlie and the other boys dressed in their best suits for inspection by their guardian. With his landing card in his hand, Charlie filed down the gangplank after the others into a holding shed where they were told to strip to their underwear for a physical examination. The Canadian air was freezing and there was a great deal of complaining as a doctor's cold hands moved over each shivering boy.

Finally, their landing cards were stamped and the boys taken to the train station with their trunks. A kind Canadian woman gave every boy a packed lunch for the first part of the on-land journey. The girls had passed through another shed and were boarding trains to a different part of Canada.

The boys' train trip took two days, but Charlie didn't mind one bit. At least he wasn't on a rocking ship! He and the other boys sprawled on the wooden coach seats and fell asleep to the rhythmic clacking of the metal wheels on the track. When daylight came, Charlie looked out on solid pine forests as the train chugged its way through Quebec and then Ontario. The land looked nothing like the tidy English countryside he'd seen on his trip up to London.

Another night on the hard seats and the group arrived at the train station in Toronto. It was enormous and noisy, with tracks and trains and people coming and going in every direction. The weary boys collected their trunks and walked outside where they were told to climb up on a horse-drawn wagon for the ride to the Canadian Distributing Centre at 214 Farley Avenue.

☞ All aboard for the ride to the Distributing Centre in Toronto where the boys will rest for a few days before being assigned to their workplaces.

The superintendent of the Home, Alfred Owen, was a friendly man who welcomed the boys and assigned them to the dormitories. He told them they'd have a few days to recover from the journey before he'd assign each of them to their new home. This was not an easy task, Mr. Owen said. For every Home Boy who arrived, there were at least ten requests from Ontario farmers looking for help.

Three days later, on March 15, Charlie signed an agreement to work for a farmer named N. Slinger at Inkerman, a small town in the Ottawa Valley, northeast of Toronto.

A New Home in Canada

At two o'clock the next afternoon, Charlie was taken by a man from the Centre and put on another train for the five-hour trip to Inkerman. Mile after mile, sitting beside strangers who ignored him, Charlie stared out the window at fields, wide rivers, and stretches of leafless trees. This flat, bare land was to be his new home. Although it was still early in the trip, Charlie was hungry. He devoured the cheese sandwiches and biscuits and drank the cold tea they'd sent with him from the centre. The afternoon hours went on, Charlie dozed and woke hungry, angry at himself for not saving some of the lunch. It was dark when the conductor came to announce the stop at Inkerman. The train pulled into the station, and the conductor handed down Charlie's trunk wishing him the best of luck.

Standing on the deserted platform in the dark, Charlie watched the train pull away, leaving behind a thin trail of white smoke in the freezing night air. Charlie shivered and looked around. There was no one on the platform, nothing but solid black in every direction. Charlie inspected the empty station office. There was no one to ask about the farmer who was supposed to be coming to pick him up. He paced the platform and peered around the corner of the building into the darkness, then moved back to stand under the only light.

The Agreement

An indentured worker is one who is bound by a contract or agreement to work for another person. In March of 1912, sitting in the office at the Canadian Distributing Centre in Toronto, Charlie was shown a paper stating that he would work for a Canadian farmer until he turned eighteen. In exchange, he would receive his board, lodging, clothing, and necessities. He would be allowed to attend school until he reached the age of fourteen.

The employer would pay him one dollar a month and an annual fee of fifteen dollars was to be sent to the Distributing Centre. It would be held in an account in Charlie's name at the Canadian Bank of Commerce in Toronto until he turned twenty-one.

Charlie was thirteen years old. He signed.

Charlie was thirteen years old and alone somewhere in a huge, strange country. The Barnardo boys in Toronto had scattered to farms all over Ontario. His dear family was halfway around the world. Charlie slumped down beside his trunk, his back against the wall. He'd decide what to do when morning came.

Charlie woke to the sound of a raspy voice calling his name. Dimly he made out a horse and wagon at one end of the station platform and a tall man with a cap pulled low over his eyes stomping toward him. The man grunted that unless Charlie felt like spending the rest of the night on the station platform, he'd better get himself and his trunk on the wagon fast. Charlie didn't like the sound of Mr. Slinger, but he had to go with him. Charlie scrambled to his feet, pushed his trunk across the platform and into the back of the wagon and climbed in front beside this rough man who was to be his new boss. Mr. Slinger snapped the reins to get the horse moving and they rode in total silence for half an hour. Then, at another sharp crack of the reins, the horse headed down a slope, made a turn and stopped.

One light showed in a window of the farm house. Inside, the farmer's wife was wrapped in a dressing gown. Mrs. Slinger was as short as her husband was tall; her face was pinched and grey and her eyes avoided Charlie's as she pointed to a cot in a rough boarded room at one end of the outside porch.

Too tired to unpack, Charlie lay down on the cot in his travelling suit and folded the jacket for a pillow. The lumpy mattress smelled of mouldy straw. He reached to pull the thin blanket around his shoulders. The Slingers were talking inside the kitchen and Charlie overheard Mr. Slinger. That kid's too small, he said. No use at all for the heavy farm work around here.

The night air flowed over Charlie through the cracks in the wallboards. He rolled over so his back was to the draft, but it didn't help. He was still bitterly cold. Cold and alone. After all the travel and the excitement that came with it, he could hardly believe that this was where his mother wanted him to be—a farmhouse in the middle of nowhere with two unfriendly people. For the first time since he'd left his mother, Charlie had an attack of homesickness. He squeezed his eyes shut but couldn't stop the tears.

He shivered and cried, then after a while, wiped his face with the tail of his shirt and talked sharply to himself. Like it or not, this was his new life. He'd signed a paper promising to work for this man and that was the way it had to be. He'd show the Slingers. He could work as hard as anyone. Charlie fell asleep with the words of the governor at Leopold House running through his head: *Work hard and learn all you can. There are great opportunities waiting in the new land.*

And Hard Work There Was

On the first morning, Mr. Slinger took Charlie to a field where two huge work horses stomped restlessly in the icy air.

There was a mean look in Mr. Slinger's grey eyes as he told Charlie he'd have to learn to harness the horses and plow the two large fields for spring planting,

Charlie watched as Mr. Slinger buckled a collar on one horse, then lifted a heavy harness onto his shoulder and tossed it over the animal's back, fastening the bit in the horse's drooling mouth. He pulled what he called the "breeching" over the huge rump of the first horse, and reached under its sagging stomach to fasten another strap. Next horse is yours, he said to Charlie.

Everything about the horses terrified Charlie, from their yellow teeth, longer than piano keys, to their enormous twitching flanks level with his eyes. He could just balance the harness on his shoulder but he couldn't manage to throw it over the horse. He tried again and again but he wasn't tall enough.

Cursing angrily, Mr. Slinger grabbed the heavy harness and threw it roughly onto the horse's back. The animal snorted and reared so that Charlie had to jump to avoid a kick from its thick hooves. This seemed to further infuriate Mr. Slinger, who showed the first taste of his temper by reaching over to smack Charlie sharply on the shoulder.

A metal plow attached to a pole lay nearby in the dirt. Mr. Slinger drove one horse over the pole, then fastened a neck yoke to each horse to keep them apart. He picked up the reins and the handles of the plow, slapped the horses with the reins, and tipped the plough into the ground, to start a narrow furrow. After a few minutes he snarled at Charlie to take his place, telling him to get on with it and to keep the furrows straight. Hands on his hips, the farmer watched Charlie's first clumsy attempts before shaking his head and stomping away.

Charlie had no idea he'd have to deal with such big, smelly animals and do such heavy work. After just an hour, he was exhausted. He struggled on as best he could with the hard work of keeping the team moving forward, then turning at the border of the field to head back, all the time trying to keep the furrows in straight lines.

He worked all day without a break and at night was too exhausted to help Mr. Slinger unhitch the team before stumbling into his hard bed on the frigid porch.

The next morning, Mr. Slinger left Charlie alone to harness the horses. He knew he had to find a way to do it. Grabbing a wooden box from the barn, Charlie put it beside the horse and stood on it. It worked. That was one problem solved, but now Charlie had to watch that the larger horse, who was always turning his head to bare his teeth, didn't find a way to bite him.

Hour after hour, day after day, Charlie worked the fields. Finally, when all the sod was turned and the two fields black with thick rich soil, Charlie waited for Mr. Slinger to tell him he'd done a good job. The simple praise never came. Instead, Mr. Slinger snapped that he'd better be ready to work smartly with the disk harrow the next day. *

Working the Fields in 1912

When he arrived in Canada, Charlie knew nothing about preparing a field for planting. His first lesson was to get over his fear of the two big work horses. Once he'd learned to harness them, he had to hitch the team to a walking plough. He stood behind the plough holding both handles. With no spare hand to hold the reins, Charlie was told to loop them around his neck. He had to be careful not to choke as the horses moved forward and the plough-share (the iron point) dug into the soil to form rows called furrows.

The next stage, known as disking, was when Charlie had to go over the fields again with the horses pulling a disk harrow. The row of sharp metal disks cut through the furrows, breaking up the dirt and smoothing the field to make it ready for planting.

FIVE

More Hard Work

Charlie had no idea what a disk harrow was, but he soon found out. Long into the next day Charlie led the horses back and forth dragging the heavy metal disks until the entire field was smooth. Then, with not a word passing between them, Charlie and Mr. Slinger walked up and down the rows scattering oat seeds from bags slung over their shoulders.

Once the plowing and seeding were finished there was still the daily work. One of Charlie's important jobs was to empty the ashes from the large cooking range in the kitchen and keep up the supply of chopped firewood. The stove burned all day to heat the house and keep the oven warm so Mrs. Slinger could cook her miserly meals. It did not seem fair after all his work that she gave him such terrible food—watery porridge for breakfast, then potatoes, cabbage, and more potatoes. Charlie was always hungry and waited in vain for some of the meat she gave Mr. Slinger. Still, after a few weeks, Charlie could feel himself growing stronger; his legs seemed longer and at night he'd secretly test the new muscles in his arms.

It was also Charlie's job to help milk the farm's thirty-two cows twice a day. At five in the morning the sleepy boy followed Mr. Slinger into the barn filled with the smells of warm cattle. Perched on a short stool with his shoulder and cheek resting on a cow's huge belly, Charlie practiced until he'd learned to squirt steady streams of milk into a tin bucket. The plunking of the milk against the tin and the gentle mooing of the cows were the only comforting sounds in Charlie's new world. It was

 ☞ Disking fields was hard work for a thirteen-year-old boy like Charlie.

good to be out of the way of the nasty horses and the snarling Mr. Slinger, who cuffed or slapped when he was angry.

At night, when Charlie was too tired and hungry to think, the cows had to be milked again. More than once, an angry Mr. Slinger woke Charlie by a sudden jab after the boy had fallen asleep with his head slumped against a cow. In a rage, the farmer would cuss Charlie as a stupid orphan boy. Charlie would do his best to ignore the hurtful words. He knew he wasn't stupid, and he wasn't an orphan either. He also knew that neither of the Slingers cared enough to ask what had happened to his family.

Charlie's mother wrote faithfully every month, even though the postage was expensive. Her letters told him she'd finally been allowed a visit with his sisters Freda and Edie in the girls' orphanage in Southampton, but there was still no news of Arthur. Charlie's chest ached when he thought about his brother. He hoped Arthur would soon learn to write so he'd know how things were. He wondered if anyone ever gave him a sweet. One of the boys at Barnardo's had told Charlie that Fegan's boys were often beaten, something that would never happen at Barnardo's.

Charlie didn't want his mother to be concerned about him, so in his own letters, he tried to find good things to say about his life. He told her how the Slingers took him by horse and buggy to the church at Inkerman on Sunday mornings. He mentioned meeting two other Barnardo boys who worked on nearby farms and how they'd hang around the gravestones in the churchyard after the service, telling each other about their employers. One of the boys worked for a sick, old widow and he looked even more worn out than Charlie from all the work he had to do. The other had an easy time with kind people who talked about adopting him. These meetings were Charlie's only opportunity to talk to anyone his own age. What he didn't tell his mother was that he'd be lonelier than ever after saying goodbye to the boys each Sunday.

Spring was relentlessly hot that year. The worst part of Charlie's days was not that he was scared of the horses, or worried that he'd chop his leg instead of the firewood. It wasn't his hard bed on the drafty porch or that there was never enough food. The worst part was that the Slingers were so nasty. The hitting wasn't so bad, but they belittled his English accent, saying he spoke funny and called him lazy. Charlie wanted to yell back that he wasn't lazy, and that he couldn't help his accent. In the end, though, he kept his thoughts to himself. He'd be beaten if he spoke out.

Charlie knew that, according to the agreement he'd signed at the Distributing Centre, children under fourteen were entitled to attend school. He tried to persuade Mr. Slinger and then Mrs. Slinger to let him go, pointing out that he was still thirteen. He'd turn fourteen in August, he argued, and this was his last chance. But the Slingers refused, saying he was needed for work at this busy time on the farm.

The Slingers didn't even bother to mention his birthday when August rolled around. Charlie had shown them the birthday letter he'd received from his mother a week earlier, but the Slingers didn't care enough to say a word to him on the day.

For a moment, in early September, Charlie thought his ordeal might be over. A neighbouring farmer came by to help Charlie and Mr. Slinger cut the oats. He seemed a kind enough man, especially compared to Mr. Slinger, who for some reason was in a fury those days and yelled at Charlie more than ever. One day he'd even struck at Charlie's head with a harness strap. The neighbour saw it all and Charlie hoped he might speak to Mr. Slinger, but the man left at the end of the week without saying a word about what he'd seen. The next week, though, the neighbour came back to the house to invite Charlie to see his new colt, who was just a few months old. Charlie walked over to the farm that evening and the neighbour's wife took his photograph with the beautiful little horse.

☞ Charlie sent this photograph of himself with
the neighbour's colt home to his mother.

Winter on the Farm

The first snowfall came early in October that year and surprised Charlie when he stepped outside to lead the steaming cows to pasture. This was the Canada he'd imagined, with the fields all white and the snow-laden trees looking like a Christmas card. Charlie made his first snowballs, hurling them over the cows, and thought how Arthur would laugh like crazy to see him throwing snowballs over the backs of Canadian cows.

Then the Canadian winter really set in. The snow piled up level with the window ledges, once keeping the door from opening. Every night, Charlie shivered in the makeshift room on the freezing porch. He tried stuffing the spaces between the boards with newspaper, but the frost crept in anyway. He wore all his clothes to bed, but woke up shaking. In the dark, he'd reach for the only thing he had from his family—his father's bottle opener. Holding it in his hands under the covers he'd try to remember what life had been like when his father

was alive. Yes, they'd been poor and sometimes cold, but there had always been jokes and time to play. If only his father hadn't caught pneumonia, the family would still be together, all of them above the sweet shop in England.

In the mornings, Charlie forced himself to get up and start a fire with the kindling he'd laid beside the stove the night before. He washed in water so icy he sometimes had to break the frozen crust on the surface of the bucket. Long before dawn, light appeared in the eastern sky through the kitchen window and the Slingers came stiffly down from their bedroom. Charlie would be sitting in front of the range in his jacket, overalls and cap. Instead of being pleased to find Charlie ready to go, Mr. Slinger would growl that a hired boy should be out in the barn milking instead of wasting good wood in the fire.

In January of that difficult winter, Charlie came down with a cold that wouldn't go away. Mrs. Slinger complained that his coughing sounded like a barking dog and it was keeping her awake at night, but she did give him an extra blanket, unfortunately every bit as thin as the other one. It was during those days that Charlie missed his mother the most. She'd always known how to make her children feel better, and Charlie longed for the touch of her soft hands on his forehead. But his mother was an ocean away. ✳

SIX

A Fresh Start

One day in March, almost a year after he'd arrived at the farm, Charlie came in from the fields and saw a city man with a bushy beard sitting at the kitchen table with the Slingers. The man introduced himself as Mr. Armstrong, an inspector from the Barnardo's Centre in Toronto. The Home boys had been told that someone would come to check on them, but Charlie was worried that perhaps Mr. Armstrong was there because the Slingers had complained.

Charlie had a decision to make. He wanted to tell the inspector about not having enough to eat, about not being allowed to go to school, and about Mr. Slinger's hitting, but if he did he knew things could be much worse after the inspector left.

Mr. Armstrong turned to Charlie and asked how he was doing. Charlie paused, thought about the consequences and gave his answer: He was fine. But the look on his face made Mr. Armstrong ask another question. How did Charlie like the work on the Slinger farm? Charlie barely had a chance to say anything before he started coughing and couldn't stop.

Mr. Armstrong asked to see where Charlie slept and followed him to the roughly boarded porch. He sat on the cot, running his fingers through his beard, and looked Charlie in the eye. You can tell me, lad, he said. There was something about the man that Charlie decided he could trust. He told Mr. Armstrong everything. The man listened and nodded, without smiling, then gave Charlie a pat on the shoulder. The inspector went back into the house, shook hands with Mr. Slinger and left for

Toronto. Charlie was certain he'd made a mistake. After all, you shouldn't tell tales about your boss. But he had, and now Mr. Armstrong would probably put a poor report on him in the Toronto records.

Exactly eight days later, a team and wagon driven by a man Charlie didn't know came to the door of the Slinger farm. Mr. Slinger was out in the field and Charlie was just getting ready to scrub the outhouse—the worst job the Slingers ever told him to do. The stranger said he'd been sent by the Distributing Centre in Toronto to pick Charlie up. Charlie was being sent to work for another farmer—a Mr. Corbin—thirty miles the other side of Inkerman. Mrs. Slinger stayed upstairs as Charlie quickly put his clothes in his trunk and loaded it on the wagon. The bottle opener was safe in his pocket as he climbed up on the seat. No one said goodbye, no one thanked him for his work, and no one paid the money he was owed for his year's work.

Let them clean up their own outhouse, Charlie thought, turning away from the farm.

A Real Family

As soon as he arrived at the Corbin farm, Charlie could see they were very different people from the Slingers. Mrs. Corbin had her hair tied back in a bun, which reminded Charlie of his own mum, except that Mrs. Corbin was plump and his mum was thin. John Corbin was the kind of man who always had a half smile on his face, and, best of all, there were twin six-year-old girls called Millie and Eunice. With their braids flipping as they tore around the place, the girls reminded Charlie of his own sisters.

Mr. Corbin grew vegetables and fruit in a three-acre field at the side of the house. Rows of fruit trees bordered the long field, and a small creek ran beside the house. There was a milk cow, a bunch of chickens, and a friendly young horse called Robbie to pull the wagon. Robbie was every bit as easy to lose your heart to as the little colt Charlie had his photo taken with the autumn before. Charlie's new bedroom was in the attic, which collected heat from downstairs and was always warm. But the biggest difference between the Corbin farm and the Slinger's was that there was lots of laughing at the Corbin's—just what you'd expect with twin girls.

Charlie's arrival coincided with the arrival of spring planting in the big vegetable garden. He found that digging with a pitchfork beside Mr. Corbin was the kind of work he enjoyed. He was happy not to be driving those nasty horses through the fields at the Slinger's, and glad he wouldn't have to milk all those cows twice a day. Here, Charlie could talk a bit, sometimes about his family, as he worked alongside Mr. Corbin.

As the weather warmed, Charlie planted rows of carrots, beans, peas, turnips, and corn. He learned how to hill up potatoes and how to stake up the beans. Every day Charlie and the twins fed the chickens and gathered eggs, and with only one cow to milk, there was always time to play hide-and-seek, show the girls how to sail paper boats down the creek, and to lift them up

☞ On the way to sell vegetables and fruit at the Saturday market.

on Robbie for rides around the farm. Sometimes Charlie helped Mrs. Corbin in the kitchen and after dinner he washed the dishes while the girls dried, giggling and teasing him the whole time. They'd just started school and Charlie helped with their reading. He was fourteen now and deeply regretted that his years at school were finished, but there were lots of books at the Corbin farm and he could read at night. Now there was much to tell his mother in his weekly letters.

Charlie was astonished to see the seeds he'd planted come shooting out of the ground so quickly, and by mid-June radishes, onions, and baby carrots were ready to pick and load on the wagon to sell at the Saturday market. All summer the twins rode to town with Charlie and Mr. Corbin. The girls turned out to be real hawkers—holding up bunches of carrots and radishes and bragging to customers about the fat green peas and juicy tomatoes. The Corbin's stall always seemed to sell out before any of the others.

After he'd loaded the empty crates back on the wagon, Charlie would take the twins to the general store where they could spend their weekly allowance of five cents. Under the glass counter were rows of sweets, which Eunice and Millie called candy. Everytime they went to the store, Charlie remembered how his father had always passed out handfuls of treats to his children. He told the twins how funny Arthur used to look with a big gobstopper stuck in his bulging cheek.

One of the great things about being at the Corbin's was that Mrs. Corbin loved to cook. Sometimes Mr. Corbin took Charlie fishing near their farm and they'd bring home fat trout for Mrs. Corbin to fry. She roasted chickens, and made delicious custard puddings and fresh biscuits to go along with the vegetables. In midsummer, Charlie had his first taste of corn on the cob, and the juicy cobs dripping with butter became his instant favourite. In August, on his fifteenth birthday, the family had a surprise party with a cake and presents. After a feast of corn, there were strawberries from the garden to go with the cake.

Belonging

Two years went by quickly, and always, Mrs. Corbin and the girls were interested to hear about Charlie's family in England. When letters came they were passed around. Arthur was nearly nine and could send his own letters now. Charlie was upset to read that the boys on the playground sometimes bullied his brother. Arthur wrote that if he didn't eat his gummy porridge for breakfast, he'd be made to eat it for dinner. He said he could hardly wait to come to Canada but he wasn't sure if he'd qualify for Fegan's program to send boys overseas. Charlie had heard that boys had to be a good size and physically strong to qualify to come to Canada, and he worried that Arthur was probably still small for his age. Millie and Eunice worried along with Charlie.

The news from Freda and Edie was that they'd left the orphanage and, like their older sisters, were working "in service" at local hotels. His mother had a new job as a laundress at Claremont Lodge, a large private home in Southampton. Nellie was turning four and almost ready to start school.

Charlie missed them all, but more and more, he felt he was in the right place. Taking the farm's produce to the town market was his favourite job because now Mr. Corbin let Charlie drive Robbie with the cart himself. In July, Charlie picked baskets of juicy plums and bags of potatoes to sell. In September, he loaded up bushel baskets of apples and pears that always sold out. Afterwards, he'd meet some of his Barnardo friends. One of them had word that Charlie's friend Peter, the photographer who'd winked at him at Barnardo's, was working in Manitoba, but there was never a way to contact him. Once Charlie caught a glimpse of the Slingers walking across the street but he pretended not to see them. He didn't want to think about the unhappy year he'd spent shivering on their drafty porch.

In the mornings, Mrs. Corbin was up before Charlie. She lit the fire in the range and had water boiling for tea before he even came down to the kitchen. Charlie always made certain she had enough wood and prided himself that he chopped all the pieces the same size so the fire would burn evenly. It was never too much work to do special things for Mrs. Corbin.

In the early fall, when he and Mr. Corbin spent several days in the bush cutting wood for the winter, Charlie realized for the first time that he was every bit as strong as Mr. Corbin. He was almost six feet tall now and had calluses on his hands that proved he worked hard. He felt very grown up working a long day beside his employer.

Mr. Armstrong, the inspector from Toronto, had been to the Corbin farm twice. Right in front of Charlie, the Corbins said that Charlie was a hard worker and a very intelligent boy. Mr. Corbin told the inspector he couldn't think how he'd manage without Charlie's help. The girls teased Charlie by telling the inspector that he was mean because he wouldn't let them jump on his bed. When Mr. Armstrong stroked his beard and turned to Charlie, asking how he liked living with the Corbins, Charlie told him things were good. He grinned and grabbed for the twins, teasing that everything would be perfect if he wasn't living with two noisy monkeys!

That night, when Charlie settled under the covers in his warm room overlooking the creek he felt truly happy. He belonged here with his second family. ✳

☞ Charlie on the porch at the Corbin farm.

SEVEN

The World Is at War

It was 1914—Charlie's fourth year on the Corbin farm, and the year of his seventeenth birthday—and rumours were flying about the possibility of war in Europe.

In July, the Germans invaded Belgium and the British prime minister demanded that Germany withdraw. The German government refused, and at 11 p.m. on August 4, 1914, King George V signed a Declaration of War against Germany. As part of the British Empire, Canada was also at war.

Very soon, five million British men had enrolled in the armed forces, and in Canada, hundreds of young men eighteen and older were rushing to sign up for overseas service.

All through the days of that long winter there was excited talk on the farm about the war. Over the dinner table and in town

Charlie heard stories about the fierce battles being fought by British troops in France. The first zeppelin bombed London, causing many casualties, and Charlie worried that his family might be bombed, too. He thought hard about what he should do. He knew he was needed on the Corbin farm, but he was strong and healthy and it was only right he do his part to fight for Britain. He made a decision. On his eighteenth birthday he'd enlist in the Canadian army.

Charlie turned eighteen in August of 1915. He was eager to sign up, but Mr. Corbin asked if he'd consider staying on another few months to see the farm through the fall. Charlie agreed, and for the last time he took baskets of fruit and vegetables to the Inkerman market, gave the twins rides on Robbie, and received an extra helping of

The Great War

This name was given to World War I, which began on August 4, 1914, and ended at 11 a.m. on November 11, 1918. At the start of the war, Canada was a country with fewer than eight million people. So strong was the support for Britain that 430,000 men and women in Canada signed up to serve (2,500 women worked as nurses in dressing stations, which were often dangerously close to the front lines).

There were 6,211 Barnardo boys who fought in the war, 514 of whom would lose their lives. Charlie was one of the lucky ones.

At the end of four years of fighting, almost ten million men on both sides had been killed and many more were wounded, crippled for life or left with shattered nerves. More than 60,000 of the dead were Canadians.

Mrs. Corbin's apple pie. On November 19, with the farming done for the season, Charlie went into town to sign his attestation papers. He wrote home to tell his mother that he was now a private in the 77th Battalion of the Canadian Expeditionary Force.

Like all the young men who signed up, Charlie knew it was possible he might die on the battlefield, but dying was not something young men took too seriously in those first days of the war. Fighting for your country was the right thing to do, and going to war along with other soldiers was exciting. Still, Charlie had no idea what it would be like to kill German boys, most of them his own age, and he hoped he'd never have to.

On his last day at the farm, Charlie dressed in the infantry's worsted tunic and high marching boots. He shook hands with Mr. Corbin, who said he was sorry he was too old to sign up himself. Charlie accepted a tearful kiss from Mrs. Corbin and let the twins hug him a hundred times. They ran along the platform after the train as Charlie leaned out the window to wave a last goodbye.

Charlie settled back in his seat for the trip to Kingston, Ontario, where recruits took their training. As a new soldier he slept in a barracks bunk, marched five hours a day with a heavy pack, and learned to fire a shiny .303 rifle with the attached bayonet. For the first time in his life, Charlie was earning real money and he requested that his pay of fifteen dollars a month be sent directly to his mother in Southampton. The money would make a big difference to her and to Nellie.

Seven months later, when Charlie had completed his training, he sailed with his new army buddies from Halifax to Liverpool. Tucked inside his heavy duffle bag, going back to England with him as a lucky talisman, was his father's black bottle opener. Soon he'd see his own family again! He'd find out if his mother had been receiving his army pay, and he could travel up to Stony Stratford to see Arthur at Fegan's and make sure his brother wasn't being mistreated.

The boat trip was not as rough as his trip to Canada five years before, but Charlie

☞ Charlie proudly wearing his uniform with the Canadian Expeditionary Force in 1915.

still suffered from seasickness and was glad to see England's trim and tidy green fields. On his arrival at the Liverpool barracks, Charlie was handed a notice that he was being transferred to the 28th Battalion. He'd soon be shipping off to France.

Charlie's life was to be changed by a battle that began on July 1, just two days later. His Canadian unit was still safe in England when the first British soldiers clambered out of the trenches onto the battlefield in the French Somme valley. On the first day of what became known as the Battle of the Somme, an astounding 58,000 British troops were killed or wounded, setting a one-day record as the greatest disaster in military history.

Word of the tragedy spread quickly among the newly arrived Canadian troops. All leave was cancelled—a great disappointment for Charlie who would not be allowed to see his mother and sisters or Arthur after all. For Charlie it was frustrating to be so near his family, and not able to visit them, but the new recruits were told they needed more weeks of heavy training to be ready for their first overseas battle.

At the Front

On August 14, the 28th Battalion sailed from Plymouth across the English Channel to Le Havre in France, and Charlie had his first look at the damage done by trench warfare. What had once been rolling hills with crops of corn and sugar beets was now a treeless wasteland of craters and mud. The land looked dead. Their battalion was taken by horse-drawn wagons to their position in the sand-bagged trenches. Along with hundreds of other soldiers, always cold and wet, Charlie waited for the order to attack. After days of deafening bombardments pounding the earth around them, a whistle, exactly like the one at Barnardo's, sounded down the line. At the signal, shoulder to shoulder with his new buddies, Charlie tightened the hold on his rifle, and for the first time, climbed up the side of the trench, into the territory called no man's land.

The Battle of the Somme

Things had not gone well for the British and French in the first years of the war. In the summer of 1916, a new offensive known as The Big Push was planned toward the German front near the river Somme in France. The Canadian Expeditionary Force was placed under the command of General Douglas Haig of the British army.

As wave after wave of soldiers left the trenches they made easy targets for the forewarned German machine gunners. Throughout the summer and into the fall, there continued to be a terrible loss of lives.

Advances were slow but finally, in early November, the German fortress at Courcelette was captured. After forty hours of continuous fighting, the treacherous Regina Trench was taken on November 11, but when the weather worsened, the battle was called off on November 18 – just one day after Charlie was wounded.

The Battle of the Somme lasted four and a half months and gained only ten kilometres of ground. The toll was especially heavy for the Canadians who fought in the battle. More than one quarter of the men were killed.

The Battle of the Somme was rightly called a blood bath, but it did serve to solidify the reputation of the courageous Canadian infantry as a highly respected fighting force.

☞ Bayonets at the ready, tension is high for the waiting soldiers.

Bullets shrieked above his head as Charlie and the other soldiers struggled forward through knee-deep mud. The German attack stayed strong, sending a steady hailstorm of gunfire that again and again forced the Canadians back to the safety of their trench.

Exhausted, Charlie tried to sleep, still in his uniform and helmet, his heavy ammunition pouches shifted to one side. Once darkness fell, the trench was invaded by hoards of what the soldiers called corpse rats. Charlie woke to see beady rodent eyes skittering over his sprawling mates, the rats' long tails whipping against the men's faces. Most nights, enemy shells lit up the sky, and sometimes—lying awake and tired beyond belief—Charlie wasn't sure if it was day or night.

Usually the arrival of the supply wagons announced the morning, but on many days the wagons couldn't make it through, and there was not even a mug of hot tea or a tot of rum to give the soldiers courage to go on. Still, the dreaded whistle sounded, and once again Charlie and his mates stumbled up and over the rim of the trench. Some days, the landscape was so filled with smoke that Charlie could barely see the men beside him. Once, he slipped on something in the mud and realized his foot had rolled on a dead man's arm. It was hideous nightmare that Charlie would never forget.

He staggered on, desperately hoping the sweep of machine-gun fire wouldn't find him. Beside him, the sudden thwack of a bullet cracked into the neck of a comrade, flipping the man up and back, where he lay dead in the mud.

His heart thudding with fear, Charlie trudged on, bent over at the waist, his rifle pointing ahead, his feet rubbed raw inside his soaked boots, his eyes and throat stinging, his brain turning him into an unthinking robot. And once again the Canadian battalion was turned back.

☞ Soldiers waiting for the whistle signal to go over the top at the Battle of the Somme.
☞ First aid treatment for wounded soldiers in WWI trenches saved many lives.

Day after day, the futile attacks went on until, in mid-September, the infantry were issued more efficient rifles, and twenty-four of the first tanks ever used in warfare were brought in to support the battle. All through the next weeks, even though the tanks proved useless, small, slow advances were made. By mid-November, Charlie's battalion had captured the bombed-out town of Courcelette. Beyond the town was a fortress they'd named Candy Trench, where there had once been a French sugar refinery. In another difficult attack, the Canadian battalion finally captured Candy Trench. At last Charlie was able to rest and celebrate the victory with his buddies. That night, he fell asleep dreaming of his boyhood in Southampton, not far away across the English Channel.

Within a day of the victory, however, the men were given orders to move on to Regina Trench, the Canadian name for a long, seemingly unbeatable, German stronghold. Just after dawn on November 17, with heavy sleet and snow making it hard to walk, Charlie was moving forward, straining to see through the white blizzard in front of him. The next minute a searing pain knocked the gun from his hands, throwing him onto his stomach with his face in frozen mud. He had been shot. *

EIGHT

Back to England

Charlie didn't remember being taken in a Red Cross ambulance to the field hospital behind the front line. His first thought when he gained consciousness was that there was a searing pain in one arm. If he could hurt this much, he figured, he must be alive. Charlie opened his eyes and looked around. He was in a hospital bed, and a doctor was bending over him. The doctor explained that a German bullet had broken Charlie's right elbow and ripped through the muscle of his upper arm. He'd need surgery, and afterward would be moved to the Canadian Casualty Centre ninety miles away, near the French port of Le Tréport.

The next time Charlie woke, a heavy cast covered his arm from his shoulder to his wrist. He was in a ward with forty other wounded soldiers, and word was spreading quickly that they'd soon be shipped back to England. No one was sorry to be leaving the hell of the trenches, but they also knew they'd be sent back to fight in France when they recovered. For many days while he recuperated, Charlie's only thoughts were about seeing his family in England. After ten long days, Charlie and the others were taken by ship across the English Channel and moved into a convalescent hospital in Southampton—his hometown. Charlie couldn't believe his luck.

Charlie's mother had been notified that her son was injured and was now back in Southampton. She rushed to see him on her first day off from work at the hotel. Charlie would always remember the sight of his frail-looking mother hurrying down the ward. She sat on the side of his bed and held tight to his hand, saying over and over again how relieved she was that he was alive. Charlie was so happy to see her that all he could do was grin. So much had happened in the six years since he'd kissed his mother goodbye as he'd left for Barnardo's in London. He was a boy then, and now, he was a man. Old enough to fight for his country.

His mother asked if he had much pain in his arm. Charlie told her it wasn't too bad and said he'd rather talk about the Corbin farm, the Saturday market, and the fun he'd had with the twins. As his mother told him about her job at the lodge, he noticed there were dark circles under her eyes.

Reconnecting

Over the weeks Charlie's arm healed well, and soon he was given a day's leave to spend with his eldest sister, Hilda, and Arthur. Arthur, now eleven, had a special holiday from Fegan's to meet his soldier brother. Dressed in his uniform, Charlie picked them both up at his mother's workplace. Arthur was shy at first, holding back and staring in awe at Charlie. Eventually, he came a little closer, reached up and ran his hand down the brass buttons along the front of Charlie's uniform. Charlie grinned, flipped down Arthur's cap and announced he'd buy him some sweets at the shop where their father had worked. Arthur hopped along excitedly beside Charlie as they made their way to Canton Street. They found that the shop was now run by a crabby old woman, who treated them very differently from their father.

Hilda had grown into a beautiful young woman and talked about her plans to leave the hotel and take a new job as a maid in a private home. Arthur held onto Charlie's sleeve all day, his sharp blue eyes focused on Charlie's face as he asked a million questions. Would Charlie have to go back to the front? Charlie answered that he didn't know. It would depend on the Army board's decision after his arm had fully healed. Had Charlie been scared in France?

☞ On a day's leave with Hilda and Arthur,
  Charlie had this studio photograph taken.
  Arthur's pockets are bulging with gobstoppers.

Yes, Charlie said, he'd been scared. I was scared for you too, Arthur said. His eyes widening, Arthur asked if Charlie had killed anyone but Charlie didn't want to talk about that. It was too hard to explain why young men in one country should kill the young men of another country when you hardly understood it yourself. Instead, he encouraged Arthur to talk about his days at the orphanage.

Charlie learned that things had been hard for his brother at Fegan's. He almost never had enough to eat and the boys were often beaten. Charlie worried that Arthur was still quite small for his age and he noticed that his shoes didn't match. One, a brown shoe, was much too short and the other, a black shoe, was scuffed and ripped at the side. Arthur explained that once a year all the shoes donated to the orphanage were thrown into a pile in the yard and, at a signal, the children would rush to pick out their own. By the time Arthur got to the pile, all the matching shoes that fit him were gone. It didn't matter, Arthur assured

his big brother. In a few more years, he'd be leaving Fegan's. If they wouldn't sponsor him, he'd find another way to go to Canada. Charlie could tell by the determined look on Arthur's face that he would do just that.

All afternoon Arthur couldn't seem to stop smiling, even as he stuffed his mouth with one gobstopper after another. It was a wonderful day.

Back to Canada

In the spring of 1917, the army board determined that Charlie had a 20 per cent disability in his right arm. This meant he could no longer fire a rifle and was therefore unfit for active duty. Despite the bad news about his arm, Charlie was relieved. Thanks to the German boy who'd fired the bullet that day, Charlie would never again have to fight in France. No one knew how much longer the war would go on, but Charlie was told he'd serve the rest of his time in Canada. A month later, Charlie had a sad farewell visit with his family then

☞ Charlie's discharge certificate. G.S.W. stands
   for gun shot wound.

sailed back to Canada on the SS *Sicilian*, the same ship he'd first boarded with the Barnardo boys and girls. Days of storms made it another miserable trip.

Back on Canadian soil, Charlie travelled to Kingston again, this time to appear before a medical board. He was found fit for a soldier's duties in home service, which meant he would be assigned military work in Canada. His good conduct was recognized by a promotion to the rank of lance corporal.

Charlie spent the next year and a half doing military police work at the Canadian Garrison Regiment in Kingston. He was on guard duty at the barracks on November 11, 1918, when he heard the news that peace had been declared. The soldiers at the base rushed out onto the streets, joining a country-wide celebration as they mingled with the people in the town, all of them cheering and waving flags.

Because he had fought in one of the bloodiest battles of the war, Charlie was awarded both a General Service and a Vic-

☞ A General Service medal and the Victory medal were awarded to Charlie at the end of World War I.

tory medal. That December, he received an honourable discharge from the army.

Out of uniform for the first time in three years, and carrying his pack with his good arm, Charlie took the train to the only connection he had in Canada, the Corbin family farm outside Inkerman. The girls, Millie and Eunice, had grown, but not so much that they couldn't still hang on to him, calling him their brave war hero, and showing him how much taller they were by standing against the old marks on the kitchen wall.

Charlie was given a public welcome at a special supper in the town's Iron Hall. The leading people of the district and the farm neighbours gathered to honour their local veteran, wounded at the Battle of the Somme. Charlie felt he hardly deserved the tribute, having fought at the front for barely four months. It was a great surprise when, at the end of the evening, he was presented with a purse of money that had been collected to help him make his way after the war.

But how could he earn a living? Charlie was twenty-one years old, and apart from some weakness in his right arm, he was fit for any job. The Corbins invited him to stay and work with them, but as much as he valued their kindness, Charlie no longer wished to be the hired help. Maybe he could make a living on his own, growing and selling fruit and vegetables like Mr. Corbin, but Charlie couldn't see how he'd ever have enough money to buy land.

He'd enjoyed his police duties with the army regimental police before the war ended and had heard people talking about the fine force of the Royal North-West Mounted Police. Why not sign up with them? It might be just the career for him. ✳

☞ Charlie at twenty-one, fit and ready to begin his new life.

NINE

Finding His Way

Charlie travelled to Ottawa to apply for work with the Royal North-West Mounted Police (RNWMP). Fortunately, the wound in his arm had healed well enough for him to pass the medical examinations, and Charlie was soon accepted as a new recruit.

He was sent for six months of training to the Regina Town Depot in Saskatchewan, where he learned to ride on horseback and slept alongside other recruits in a dormitory. On graduation, he was issued an impressive-looking tunic, a wide Stetson hat, and high boots. Once again, Charlie was in uniform. His first assignment was to Manitoba with the rank of constable.

☞ Constable Charlie Harvey on parade square at Regina Town Depot, 1919.

☞ Charlie, now a constable in the RNWMP, proudly sent this portrait home to his mother in Enlgand.

☞ Dormitories for the recruits were similar to
   the ones Charlie had slept in at Barnardo's.
☞ Royal North-West Mounted Police recruits
   in training on parade square in 1919.

Charlie was first posted to Portage la Prairie in Manitoba and later to Brandon. He lived in a barracks with other single men and began to enjoy police work, enforcing traffic laws, investigating robberies, and getting to know the people in small towns. He started a boys' group for street kids and was becoming a popular policeman.

Home Again

One day, after more than a year in the force, Charlie received a letter from his sister Freda. Their mother had taken ill with pneumonia. He'd wondered why he hadn't heard from her for a while and recalled how tired she'd looked when he'd last seen her. He also remembered how helpless he'd felt when his father had died so suddenly of pneumonia. His mother's life had been hard and now she was getting older and was sick. His sisters wouldn't have enough money from their work as housekeepers to support their mother, and Charlie knew he should be there to help her. But he was just getting started in police work and he hated to leave the RNWMP. Reluctantly, he made a decision and wrote to his commanding officer asking to be discharged. Charlie was allowed to buy his way out of the force for fifty dollars, a large chunk of his savings, but he was left with enough money to book passage back to Southampton.

The seas were calmer this crossing and when he didn't feel seasick, Charlie enjoyed the time on deck. He was lucky enough to spot a large pod of graceful whales. Arriving in Southampton, he went straight to the two-room flat his mother had rented.

Sarah was sitting up in bed and she smiled when she saw her oldest boy again. Charlie hugged her, noticing her frail shoulders. He moved in with his mother and Nellie, and slept on a cot in the room that served as both sitting room and kitchen. He found work as a gardener in the large grounds at Claremont Lodge. Thanks to his time at the Corbin's farm, Charlie knew about growing things and

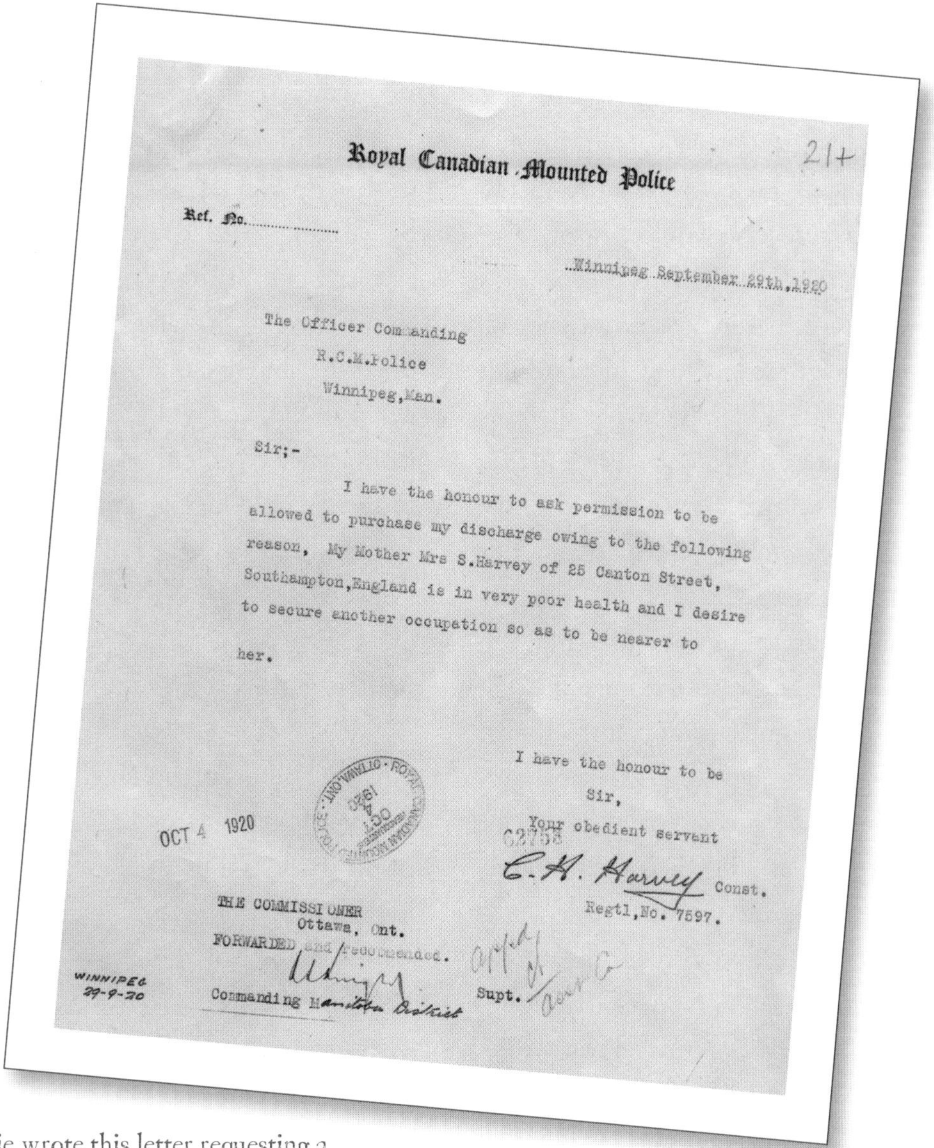

Royal Canadian Mounted Police

Ref. No.....................

Winnipeg September 29th, 1920

The Officer Commanding

R.C.M.Police

Winnipeg,Man.

Sir;-

I have the honour to ask permission to be allowed to purchase my discharge owing to the following reason, My Mother Mrs S.Harvey of 25 Canton Street, Southampton,England is in very poor health and I desire to secure another occupation so as to be nearer to her.

I have the honour to be

Sir,

Your obedient servant

C.H. Harvey Const.

Regtl.No. 7597.

OCT 4 1920

THE COMMISSIONER
Ottawa, Ont.

FORWARDED and recommended.

Supt.

WINNIPEG
29-9-20

Commanding Manitoba District

☞ Charlie wrote this letter requesting a discharge to return to England to look after his mother.

was happy tending flower beds and keeping the hedges and lawns trimmed. He found space wherever he could to grow vegetables—green onions behind the peonies and rows of radishes under the hollyhocks. He used his wages to buy food and clothing for his mother and sister. As he watched his mother become stronger and saw Nellie running and skipping with her friends, Charlie knew he was doing what his father would have wanted.

But Southampton was suffering the after-effects of the war and things in England seemed cramped compared to life in Canada. The buildings weighed in on him and Charlie found himself thinking about the open spaces around the prairie towns where he'd done police work.

His sisters came to visit on their days off and Arthur did too. Now nearly eighteen, Arthur had left Fegan's and was working two jobs—at a bakery in the daytime and a bottle factory at night. He'd made plans and was saving money to buy a passage to Canada. He told Charlie that the Canadian government would finance part of the trip and let Arthur repay the money by working for a farmer.

Arthur's big day finally came in the summer of 1923. Charlie saw his brother off at the ship dock. They promised to meet again in Canada. As Charlie walked back from the docks, he thought about his own future. Should he stay and make his life in England or should he follow his heart back to Canada?

A Final Farewell

Charlie had been back in England for five years and there was no longer any challenge in his work as a gardener. He was still living with his mother, who had found an easier job as one of the cooks at Claremont Lodge.

One day, his mother asked Charlie if he still had his father's bottle opener. Charlie took it out of his pocket to show her and she began to cry as she talked about how much Charlie's father had loved his family.

☞ Charlie's mother, Sarah Elizabeth Harvey, always kept in touch with her children.

His life was hard, she said, and he'd often talked about how he hoped things would be easier for his children. Charlie assured his mother that everything about Canada except the brief year at the Slinger's farm had been good for him. For the first time he truly understood how hard it must have been for his mother to let him go to Canada. He remembered how she'd always been hungry for news and faithful about writing to her children. It was clear how much she loved them all.

His mother wiped her eyes. You've been a fine son staying in England to help me, she said, but now you must make your own decision about where you want to be.

Charlie thought of the opportunities waiting in Canada that he'd never find in England and made his decision. His future lay across the Atlantic.

This time when Charlie left for Canada, his mother was at the dock to say goodbye. They hugged for a long time, both of them suspecting that this could be their final farewell. ✳

TEN

Life as a Mountie

Charlie was almost thirty years old when he arrived back in his chosen country. He went to stay with Arthur, who was working on a ranch outside Calgary. Charlie was hired on too and the brothers worked side by side through the winter; Arthur small and wiry, Charlie older and taller, herding cattle on a large ranch. They were a long way from Canton Street in the busy port of Southampton and they were thriving in the healthy freedom of the outdoor prairie life.

As much as he liked being with Arthur, Charlie knew after the first winter that farm life was not for him. He'd like to rejoin the RNWMP. Arthur told Charlie that he loved working on the land and planned to buy a farm of his own. They were both in Canada now, Charlie said, and they should be able to live their separate dreams.

The RCMP

Shortly after Charlie has left for England to look after his mother, the RNWMP was expanded into a national force and renamed the Royal Canadian Mounted Police (RCMP). Charlie met the requirements of being single and in good health, and was accepted into the new force as a constable. He was sent to work in the small town of Fort Qu'Appelle in southern Saskatchewan.

Charlie's first assignment was with a special squad of Mounties who were tracking down safe crackers, a gang of robbers terrorizing small towns by blowing up bank safes with dynamite. After months of work, Charlie's squad captured the gang and delivered the robbers to a Regina jail for trial.

In 1873, Canada's first prime minister, Sir John A. Macdonald, announced the formation of Canada's first police force and sent 275 mounted men west to Alberta to help open up the vast new west. The RNWMP was to establish friendly relations with First Nations tribes and make the land safe for the many agricultural immigrants arriving as settlers. This was done in a peaceful manner, earning the RNWMP great respect.

In 1920, the RNWMP was expanded into a national force and renamed the Royal Canadian Mounted Police (RCMP), adopting as its motto Maintain the Right. Charged with enforcing the law in cities and towns strung out over thousands of miles, from both coasts up to the Arctic Ocean, the new force had the largest police beat in the world.

☞ On horses of identical colour and size, the thirty-two riders of the RCMP musical ride appear in precision performances worldwide.

Today, carefully selected recruits (including women since 1974) train in Regina for twenty-four weeks. Many of the 23,000 officers have university degrees. These days it is only for ceremonial occasions that Mounties ride horses; they now use airplanes and ships, as well as trained dogs who track criminals and missing people. The modern RCMP also work with drug enforcement, computer crimes, and international agencies.

Police work is often dangerous and sometimes Mounties lose their lives in the call of duty. Unfortunately, it is also true that sometimes in protecting citizens, RCMP officers make mistakes. When this happens, Canadians have a duty, as well as a right, to challenge and review their actions, which is the only way to maintain the honourable reputation the RCMP has enjoyed for more than 135 years.

☞ Frances and Charlie are engaged.

☞ Charlie, on the right, with another officer in their winter buffalo-fur coats.

Police work was never dull and Charlie was proud to be part of a force with a reputation for "always getting their man."

It was in Yorkton, in 1933, after he had been promoted to the rank of corporal, that Charlie "got his woman." Dark-haired Frances was a stenographer in the courthouse. She'd been born on the prairies after her parents had emigrated from England. Frances and Charlie fell in love and were married the day after Christmas. A year later, they had a baby girl they called Beryl and three years after that, a boy named Bob.

Dangerous Work

In 1938, Charlie was transferred to Regina and promoted to sergeant. Winter temperatures on the Canadian prairies often fell below minus thirty degrees and one day it was reported that an elderly man had wandered outside his house and became lost in a blizzard. Charlie put on his bulky buffalo-fur coat and left with another Mountie in the patrol car to find the man. Icy roads and

☞ Digging out the car. The aftermath of a prairie winter storm.

huge snow drifts made the search dangerous and they were out most of the night. At the breakfast table the next morning Charlie, his fingers swollen and white with frostbite, told his family the good news that the man had been found alive.

Along with other Canadians, Charlie was shocked when World War II broke out. Once again, Canadians signed up to fight in Europe, but neither Arthur nor Charlie would join the fight—Charlie because he was needed for police work and Arthur because farmers were needed to keep up food supplies at home.

Both Arthur and Charlie followed the war closely. Their mother was still living in Southampton, which was heavily bombed and had terrible shortages of food. Frances and Charlie shipped parcels to Sarah regularly, and she wrote back that the tinned meats and homemade fruit cake were wonderful treats.

In 1941, the third year of the war, Charlie received the letter he'd always known would come. At the age of seventy-two, his mother had died of heart failure. Now that he had children of his own, Charlie could appreciate in a new way how difficult it must have been for his mother to put her children in orphanages. He hoped he'd never have to make that kind of decision about Beryl and Bob.

When RCMP cadets graduate, they are issued two uniforms. For everyday use, they wear a blue jacket and trousers. Their dress uniform is the brilliant scarlet tunic and full blue breeches with the yellow stripe affectionately called banana pants. A wide-brimmed felt Stetson hat, leather gloves, and tall leather boots called high browns with spurs (leftover from the days of riding horses) complete the well-recognized uniform. In addition, each police officer wears his Sam Browne, a shoulder strap and belt that holds a pistol in a leather holster. Women wear the same uniform except on formal occasions, when they wear a long skirt.

Recruits hope that over the years they will establish good work records so they will be promoted up the ranks. Starting as a constable, men and women serve for seven years before they can expect to be promoted to corporal. Some will reach the rank of sergeant and go on to become a staff sergeant.

A smaller number will be promoted as commissioned officers with the rank of inspector; even fewer become superintendents, assistant commissioners, and deputy commissioners. The final rank is to become a commissioner, who stands alone with the top job. Currently, for the first time, the commissioner has not risen through the ranks, but was appointed by the government.

☞ Officers hold their staffs proudly as they ride the superbly trained horses in the RCMP musical ride.

Up the Ranks

In 1944, Charlie was assigned to the larger town of Swift Current further west in Saskatchewan. Charlie never talked about his early life, but his children knew he'd served in the army in WWI. Every chance they got they'd climb on their father's lap and ask to see the bullet hole in his arm. Charlie would roll up his shirt sleeve so they could stare at the puckered skin around the wound. Bob said it looked like a wrinkly gopher hole. Then, knowing their dad always had some of the sweets he'd loved as a child, they'd dig for the minty humbugs in his jacket pocket.

One day, Charlie went to his top dresser drawer and brought out a black metal bottle opener to show his children. It looked very ordinary, but Charlie told them it was more than fifty years old and had belonged to their grandfather. The grandmother they had never met had given it to him when he left home at thirteen. He said he'd carried it back and forth across the Atlantic, to the battlefields in France, and to all the places he'd worked across Canada. Charlie put the opener back in the drawer, hoping some day his children might understand why it meant so much to him.

Every summer, Charlie took his family to spend his two-week holiday helping Arthur on his farm near Blackie, Alberta. Arthur had fifty cows and grew crops of wheat and oats. While Charlie and Arthur drove the combine, Beryl and Bob joined their cousins playing with the farm animals. At sunset Charlie and Arthur would stop work and come into the house for a big farm supper with corn on the cob and homemade bread cooked by Arthur's wife.

They'd reminisce around the kitchen table about the family still in England. The news from overseas was that Nellie was married and had four children and their sister Eva had moved to far-away Australia with her new husband.

When he got back home after one working holiday, Charlie wrote to Arthur:

I can't tell you how much I enjoyed my time with you. I hated to go back to work and wish I could have about two more months of haying. Bob and Beryl had the time of their lives and we're all enjoying the pies Frances made with the Saskatoon berries the children picked.

In 1945, Charlie received another promotion, this time to staff sergeant, and his family moved to Edmonton, Alberta. Charlie was invited to speak at Beryl and Bob's new school. Dressed in his scarlet tunic Charlie spoke to an assembly, telling the students about his adventures as a Mountie. He said the men in the RCMP had the best reputation for honesty of any police force in the world. He told the children they must always respect police officers and never let anyone called them "cops."

Charlie took his family to see the renowned RCMP musical ride. When his children admired the matching black horses, Charlie told them about a little colt he'd once seen and a friendly horse named Robbie he'd loved as a boy. He didn't mention two frightening work horses and an unkind farmer named Slinger.

In 1948, Charlie was promoted to inspector, moved to Ottawa, and in the spring of 1951 was transferred across the country again to Victoria in British Columbia. At fifty-four years of age, Charlie had been rewarded with a very desirable west coast posting.

☞ Charlie and Arthur working together threshing summer grain on Arthur's Alberta farm.

☞ Just after his promotion to Sergeant, Charlie sent this photo to his brother Arthur. On the back he wrote 'How much hay do you think I could pitch in this outfit?'

☞ Charlie, now an Inspector, escorted the royal
couple shortly before he retired.

☞ The beautiful young Princess Elizabeth and
her husband Prince Philip on their 1951 visit
to Canada. The coronation of the Princess
as Queen would take place in England
seventeen months later.

Escort to a Future Queen

In the fall of Charlie's first year in Victoria, Buckingham Palace announced that Princess Elizabeth and Prince Philip would tour Canada. They'd travel across the country to Vancouver Island where Charlie was the officer responsible for escorting the royal couple. So it was that the Barnardo Home Boy, who had caught a glimpse of Buckingham Palace from the top of a London tram forty years earlier, came to be the RCMP escort for the future queen and her handsome consort.

Driving up Vancouver Island with the young royals in a black convertible was an experience Charlie never forgot. Prince Philip, who was known to speed, asked to drive for the two-hour trip. Charlie didn't feel he could turn down a Prince. The trip was even more memorable when a hitchhiker attempted to hail the royal car from the side of the highway. The astounded young man watched the car, complete with the flapping royal flag, speed by him at over 160 kilometers an hour.

A Time for His Garden

In 1957, after almost thirty years in the RCMP, Charlie was awarded a silver Long Service and Good Conduct medal. It was time to retire. Charlie was a respected and well-loved officer and had a huge crowd at his retirement party. He received cards of congratulations from Eunice and Millie Corbin, who had kept in touch over the years.

By now Charlie's own children were grown and had left home. For the first time in his career, after all the moving and all the rented houses, he and Frances could finally buy their own home. They found a small house in Victoria on a double lot where Charlie had the big garden he'd always wanted. Best of all, there was a greenhouse at the back of the lot where Charlie could get an early start growing vegetables, the way Mr. Corbin had shown him so long ago.

Charlie's garden was so successful that neighours made a point of stopping by to

☞ Charlie and Frances in their Victoria garden
in 1958 with Jeremy, their first grandson.

admire the rows of potatoes and corn and the raspberry bushes. No one ever went away without a bunch of green beans, a head of lettuce, or a bag of plums. Charlie's favourite visitor was his first grandson who he carried in his arms to taste the sweet, new raspberries.

Every spring until he died, Charlie was out early in the morning preparing the soil for new seedlings. Sometimes, after a day of digging, his right arm ached from the old army wound, but he never complained. The German bullet that had kept him from being sent back to fight in France more than forty years earlier had probably saved his life.

And what an adventurous life it had been for the thirteen-year-old boy who'd bravely travelled to a new land, the lad who had worked hard on Ontario farms, the man who'd fought boldly on Europe's battlefields, and served loyally for the RCMP. It was a long way from Charlie Harvey's childhood home over the sweet shop in Southampton to this abundant vegetable garden in Victoria. It had been a fine life. *

AFTERWORD

It wasn't until I was twenty years old and went to live in England that I learned from a cousin that my father had been a Home Child. I knew he'd come to Canada from England, but not that he'd been in an orphanage. I couldn't believe it. Why hadn't my dad told me?

I telephoned Canada—a big expense in the 1950s—to ask my father. It turned out he had been worried that I would tell the story up and down our street. I was hurt at first, and then realized he was right. I would have. I thought my father's story was dramatic and even romantic. I still do. But the important thing was he didn't.

It's a sad fact that many adults who have been Home Children are ashamed of their heritage. They feel embarrassed that they were abandoned or had a parent who couldn't care for them, regret that they had to be sent away from the land of their birth, and sorrow over the mistreatment some of them suffered. Yet, almost without exception, when I talk to them I never hear regrets about their adult lives in Canada. My father loved Canada. He loved his work, his family, and his garden.

In recent years, the old policy of sending children to Canada has been harshly judged. Dr. Barnardo and other people responsible had good intentions, but the era of child emigration has long passed. It is true that when children signed on as indentured workers, they were signing an agreement they were too young to understand. Now, people feel that too many of them were exploited as child labourers, some were not well-treated or well-fed. Sadly, some children lost track of their own families forever.

My father lived from 1897 to 1961. He had two children—my brother and me—and eight grandchildren, but didn't live to see any of his eleven great-grandchildren.

Now that I have grandchildren of my own, I often wish I'd asked my father more about his childhood. I guess I was too busy with my own life to think about his. Why not ask your parents or grandparents to tell you about their early lives? Find a quiet time and ask them what they remember about the years when they were growing up. I think you'll be surprised.

As I sit here writing this, a black metal bottle opener is on the table beside me. It's old and quite ordinary, but I treasure it as dearly as I treasure the memory of my beloved father.

—*Beryl Young*

BARNARDO'S TODAY

More than 130 years (1866) have passed since Dr. Barnardo began working with children in Britain, and though the organization no longer has orphanages, it is still very active. Its motto is "Believe in Children."

Barnardo's 383 projects around the country provide help for children who are vulnerable or neglected. There are community programs for children and families in poverty, young people with disabilities, and children who have been adopted.

Before she died, Diana, Princess of Wales, was a patron of Barnardo's and she visited centres for children around England many times.

You can learn more by visiting www.barnardos.org.uk.

☞ With their motto "Believe in Children," Barnardo's helps many young people in Britain today

ACKNOWLEDGEMENTS

When I needed to find out more about my father to write this book, I contacted the Barnardo After Care Centre in England and learned that he had been a Barnardo boy. After paying a fee and waiting four months, I received an overseas package in the mail. My hands were shaking as I opened the envelope to find the earliest photograph I'd ever seen of my father, taken the day he entered the Barnardo's Home in London, a copy of his admittance form (where I learned how tall he was and how much he weighed), as well as his work history in Canada. A year later I visited the Barnardo After Care Centre in Barkingside, Ilford, England, and spent an exciting day looking through their archives to choose the photographs for this book. For their kind assistance I want to thank the Barnardo staff: Frances Brewer, Karen Fletcher, Anne Newill, Valerie Smith, Catherine Myers-Antiaye, Martine King, and Ted Trott, with special thanks to Stephen Pover, Barnardo's image librarian.

The helpful staff at Library and Archives Canada supplied information about my father's war record, including details of his medical treatment at the Battle of the Somme.

The Special Projects Section of the RCMP in Ottawa sent detailed records about my father's service with the force. As well, Carmen Harry and Shannon Cunningham in the RCMP Historical Collections Unit at the RCMP Heritage Centre in Regina answered my many questions and supplied photographs for this book.

Tim Novak, archivist at the Saskatchewan Archives Board found some wonderful winter photographs.

Gerald Edwards, himself a Home Boy and a member of the RCMP graciously shared valuable details from his own experience.

Many generous friends took time to help make this book better. I thank Roberta Rich, Shelley Hrdlitschka, Margaret Prang, Susan Moger, Maureen and Allan Thackray, Olive and Ross Johnson, Dianne Woodman, Louise Hager, Jesse Finklestein, Norma Charles, Gillian Chetty, Linda Bailey, Pat Irwin, and Jim and Heather Douglas. Madeleine Nelson was a great assistance with photographs. Anna Luckyj and Jean Wilson referred me to useful books. My cousins on the other side of the family, Frances Jenkins and Jill Jenkins, patiently taught me about horses, harrowing, and harnessing.

My brother Bob and my children, Jeremy, Margot, and Brian, read the manuscript with care. My cousins Kathy McCutcheon (Freda's daughter), Ruth McKeage (Arthur's daughter), and Dennis Eales (Eva's son) of Australia filled me in on details about our family. Jeremy Harvey (Charlie's great-grandson) lent his support and photographic skills. Myrna Harvey (Arthur's daughter) gave valuable professional help by transferring our family photographs onto disks.

Debbie Hodge, fellow writer and big-hearted friend, has been my wonderful mentor from the beginning. I am enormously grateful for the practical advice she gave me when I began to write my first book of non-fiction and for her unflagging enthusiasm when I hit a few roadblocks.

I was fortunate to have Linda Pruessen of Key Porter Books as my editor. Linda seemed to understand exactly how I wanted to tell this story and skillfully helped me to get there. Many thanks also to Sonya V. Thursby and Nina Paris at Key Porter.

I remain indebted to my agent, Beverley Slopen, for her steadfast support.

Finally, I want to thank my cousin, Phyllis Smith (Edie's daughter), who as the family archivist has inspired me with her strong interest in our family tree. For several years the email lines have been burning up between my home in Vancouver and hers in Southampton, England. Then one memorable afternoon when I visited Southampton, Phyllis and her husband Brian drove me to the street where our grandparents had lived above the sweet shop. Her daughter, Michelle Buhl-Nielson, kindly did the drawings of the sweet shop and the maps.

RESOURCES

Books

Here are some fictional stories about Home Children you'll enjoy reading:

When the Bough Breaks by Irene N. Watts (Tundra Books, 2007)

Flower by Irene N. Watts (Tundra Books, 2005)

Orphan at My Door by Jean Little (Scholastic Canada, 2001)

Film

Childhood Lost: The Story of Canadian Home Children (Telefilm Canada, 2004) is an excellent one-hour film about Home Children.

Websites

For information about family members from Britain, see www.collectionscanada.gc.ca. Follow the link for Ancestors.

For information about Barnardo's in England, see www.barnardos.org.uk. Follow the link for What we do, then the link for Working with former Barnardo's children. Or go directly to Barnardo's Making Connections email: making-connections@barnardos.org.

For contact information within Canada, see the Canadian Centre for Home Children: www.canadianhomechildren.ca.

For further information about Home Children Canada and Home Children Canada (Pacific) see www3.telus.net/home_children_Canada

PHOTO CREDITS

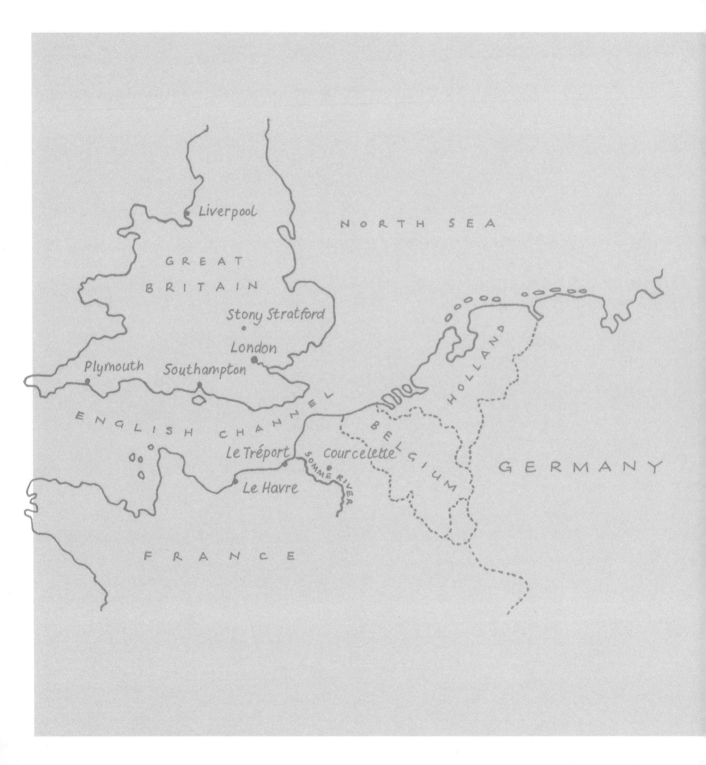